Fun, Humor & Laughter
Laughing at Everyday Life

Sharon E. Buck

FUN, HUMOR & LAUGHTER

All of the following stories are true. No disclaimers, no protecting the alleged innocent, no nothing. Fair warning though I have my attorney on retainer, on speed dial. Enjoy the following true short stories.

Copyright © 2016 Sharon E. Buck

All rights reserved.

ISBN-13: 978-0966636314

DEDICATION

To everyone who is stressed out from everyday life
and needs a good laugh.

FUN, HUMOR & LAUGHTER

NOTE TO THE READER

All of the short stories in
Fun, Humor, & Laughter - Laughing at Everyday Life
are less than 300 words. They are considered flash fiction
or in this case flash non-fiction.

Why short stories? Life is busy and crazy. You can
take a break from the stress of work, the kids hanging on you,
your partner wanting to know when dinner's going to be ready,
and change your whole attitude with ONE SHORT STORY.
Enjoy!

Is There A Parenting Book for My Parents?

When All Else Fails, Laugh

Have you ever had one of those days where everything seems to be on the downhill side of happiness and then you have lunch with a friend who is determined you can't live there? That's annoying, isn't it?

I was having lunch with a friend and wallowing in the escapades of my aging parents. She listened with sympathy, once again, and made a couple of suggestions which I promptly ignored.

She tried making a couple of jokes but I was too caught up in being the guest of honor at my own pity party to laugh. She ordered me banana pudding for desert. Yes, I ate the desert, and continued on with woe-is-me routine.

Finally she said, "Get off the cross, someone else needs the wood."

I started to laugh, then she started to laugh. Our favorite waitress Lu-Lu, yes that's really her name, came over to see what we were laughing about. We told her about getting off the cross because someone else needed the wood. She just cocked an eyebrow at us, shook her head, and we could hear her muttering, "Them two girls just ain't right."

We spent the rest of the meal just laughing at silly stuff.

Laughter is truly the best medicine.

The Happy Jar Messages

On my desk sits a medium-size clear vase with different colors of post-it notes. The notes represent good things that have happened to me. When I'm feeling a wee bit down or depressed I pull out a post-it note, read it, and remind myself of the good things that have happened. It's all about positive energy.

On a particularly frustrating day after I had already screamed at the dogs and cursed the cat's apparent Egyptian ancestry, I finally glanced up and saw my Happy Jar.

Still grumbling to myself, I put my hand in the jar and pulled out a handful of uplifting notes. Glancing at the first one, I blinked and uttered an expletive. The second one was no better. By the fourth one I started to laugh and by the sixth one I was literally almost falling out of my chair laughing.

A while back while going through a particularly aggravating situation with my elderly parents, I had written down every frustrating thought that popped into my head. Apparently not having the sense God gave a goose, I put them in my Happy Jar.

They looked pretty silly now but they served their purpose. They made me laugh, although I do suggest putting only positive notes in the Happy Jar.

Did the Candy Fairy Drop By?

There is a genetic pre-disposition in our family that one must always have hard and chocolate candy in the house at all times. This is, of course, for "guests" who may drop in to see to see my parents. Candy is rarely offered when guests drop in, including their own children; HOWEVER, it is there for them when a quick pick-me-up is needed.

Recently I had gone over to my parents' house and in the course of conversation, I absently reached into the candy dish and there…was…no…candy. No chocolate, no hard candy, no nothing. Since I had just taken my mother to the grocery store and saw her purchase two bags of candy, I knew there was some around.

"Where's the candy, Mom?"

"We don't have any candy." She smiled sweetly as only mothers can do.

"Yes, you do. I saw you buy some at the grocery store yesterday."

"We don't have any." This time with a slight edge to her voice.

I looked around the kitchen area, nothing. I couldn't imagine where she had hidden the candy. Then it dawned on me.

"Mom, did you eat all of that candy?"

"No."

"Where is it?"

My dad popped his head in the living room. "She ate it all except for two pieces."

If looks could kill, my dad would have been dead.

Mom said, "We don't have any candy."

The Clowns

One of my favorite expressions is "not my circus, not my monkey." As far as I am concerned it applies to virtually anything in life. It simply means not my problem.

I thought it was a great way for me to disengage myself from things, situations, and people that I didn't need to be involved in or with. It was actually more of a reminder for me to mind my own business and let others figure out their situation without my help.

I probably use that expression at least three times a day. I didn't realize how much it annoyed at least one of my friends until I was telling another funny story about my aging parents. She made the error of saying, "Then what happened?"

I told her and then finished with "not my circus, not my monkey."

She laughed and said, "Yeah, but they're your clowns."

Rut row! Now I have to keep the clowns under control. Unfortunately, this is also creating a brain spin. I mean, I have to now totally re-evaluate if I have any clowns running around loose on every story.

It was so much simpler before the clowns came along.

The Comeback

In our family there is a wide range in ages. We have the same set of parents and the age differences range between me and my younger sisters from two to seven years to ten and a half years.

My dad was prone to pontificate about having two crops of girls, particularly at church. I guess it was a male source of pride that he was still a producing member of society back in the day.

While at church one day, my parents were very active and it seemed like we were there every time the doors opened, my dad was once again bragging to a group of choir members and their spouses about how he had produced two crops of girls.

Everyone politely laughed…again. My dad, apparently being fueled by the laughter, pointed at me and said, "This one is getting ready to move to Miami and the youngest there is getting ready to go into middle school. Heh, heh. Two crops of girls."

My mother, probably one of the most laid back people you'll ever met, finally said, "Bill, we're not raising corn here. We're raising girls."

Deep belly laughter erupted from the group. My dad turned slightly red and dipped his head.

Never again has he ever referred to his four daughters as a crop.

Decisions, Decisions

Picking up my parents after a week's vacation at my sister's, we met for lunch. We had picked out two restaurants, giving my parents an option to choose what they wanted to eat. And therein created the problem.

We gave our parents a choice of a noodle restaurant or "Welcome to Moe's!" restaurant. My dad is not a big pasta fan and, although from Oklahoma, he doesn't particularly care for southwestern food unless it's something that meets his very rigid standards of what constitutes southwestern food.

My dad, God bless him, cannot and will not make a quick decision. He's always been this way, old age has nothing to do with it.

Finally after much debate, as my sister and I were rolling our eyes at each other, she took the initiative saying, "We can't stand here all day. Pick something out, I'll get it, and you sit down." And with that she opened the door and went inside the noodle restaurant.

On the two hour journey home, my dad complained several times that he had been rushed to make a decision on his food and he wasn't sure he had made the right decision.

Finally, my mother said, "Bill, you took ten minutes. How much longer did you need?"

He was silent the rest of the way home, although I could hear him muttering in the back seat.

I Can't Hear You!
Blah, Blah, Blah!

Dear Food Network, You Owe Me Money

Animals being hungry after watching the Food Network channel isn't a scientific study but one I've observed with my own animals, specifically my dogs.

Being the ever-loving, doting human in my precious dogs' lives, I leave the tv on for their amusement and entertainment when I leave the house. Of course, the cynical among you might opine that I'm just too lazy to walk over to the remote control and turn it off before leaving. Whatever!

I've discovered that if I leave the Food Network channel on while I'm gone, they are absolutely RAVENOUS upon my arrival. Really. To the point that they are bouncing around and dancing when I come in the door. Much as I'd to believe it's because they're excited to see me, I know in my heart of my hearts it's really only because they want FOOD…NOW!

However, when I don't leave the Food Network channel on with all of those delicious meals being prepared by celebrity chefs, the dogs are only mildly happy to see me entering the house.

Conclusion: the Food Network is causing my dogs to be beyond hungry when I come home. I wonder if they'll pay for the increased dog food costs?

Cat Amusement

My black-and-white cat Sox has dubbed himself the King of the Kitchen and he doles out precious tasty morsels to his adoring subjects, aka my two dogs, when I'm not home.

Of course, I guess this is my fault because I leave opened pouches of dog treats on the counter. It makes it easier for me to give them treats.

It also makes it very easy for a clever and smart cat to hoist his royal highness up on the counter where he then pats the open bag over, scoops out little delicious tidbits, then pushes them off the counter one by one and then watches his adoring fan club fight over each piece.

How did I, a mere mortal who unwittingly provides the entertainment, discover this? Quite by accident, let me assure you.

I walked into the kitchen one morning and discovered the cat on the counter - as much as I've tried to keep the cat off the countertop, I've no success – the dogs were sitting quietly and looking up at him with eager anticipation.

Being the ever observant individual that I am, I noticed the dog treats were scattered all over the top. The cat, caught in the act of actually pushing a treat off the counter, immediately laid down and proceeded to clean himself.

Note to self: ALWAYS close the dog treat pouch.

It's Not Really My Bed

Three animals own me. Two dogs and a cat know in their heart of hearts that I have been placed in their lives to serve them. The fact that they also give me pleasure is a side benefit.

All three sleep in my queen size bed at night. Plop-Plop, my Lhasa Apsa, sleeps at the foot of the bed. Angel, my Malti-poo, sleeps stretched out against my back and Sox, my cat, sleeps somewhat curled around my face, shoulders…oh, heck, he sleeps wherever he likes and as long as he has a paw on me somewhere he's fine.

I, on the other hand, can't turn over at night without disturbing their royal highnesses. Let me point out, they are not thrilled when I roll over on the six inches of space they have allotted me.

Angel growls and says some ugly things under her breath. Plop-Plop decides he needs to lay on at least one foot to prevent any further movement on my part. Sox stretches and pushes a paw against me to signal his annoyance at having to move a quarter of an inch.

It doesn't make any difference whether I have a king or queen size bed the fact is…it's not really my bed, I'm just allowed to sleep in it on a regular basis.

Human Jealousy

My animals are jealous.

Oh, they're fine as long as I'm not sitting on the couch watching tv, talking on the phone, or attempting to sleep at night. If I do any of those things, THEN they start jockeying to get my attention.

Watching tv – the cat curls up next to me while my Malti-poo is trying to jump up on the couch so she can lay directly on my lap. If she fails in that attempt, then she sits on the floor and talks…continuously…until I pick her up. I've let her talk for as long as thirty-five minutes and then finally picked her up.

Talking on the phone – both dogs can be asleep until the moment I start talking to someone on the phone. If the call goes more than five minutes, they suddenly decide to play tag team chase and proceed to chase each other around the house while barking at the top of their lungs.

Going to sleep at night – all three animals sleep in the bed with me. The Lhasa hops off the bed almost as soon as he gets up there. The Malti-poo and cat literally fight over who's going to sleep closest to my face. Growling and hissing at each other for several minutes is the norm every night.

Human jealousy – it's not pretty.

Love Knows No Bounds

Recently I had a nasty sinus infection along with the flu, a rotten combination of physical ailments. Riding the couch on the way to better health, I fell asleep. Vaguely aware that I was starting to perspire, my more immediate concern was that my body felt incredibly weighed down.

Struggling to open my eyes, the brief thought occurred to me that perhaps I had died and this is what death felt like. Maybe I hadn't made it to heaven yet and this is the reason why my body felt so heavy.

Finally getting one eye to open, I discovered that Sox, my cat, was laying on my chest. Angel, the Malti-Poo was casually stretched out on my lower abdomen, hip, and leg. Plop-Plop, my Lhasa, was laying on my feet. No wonder I couldn't move! The animals were smothering me with their love!

While very appreciative that my darling animals thought enough of me to keep me warm and loved during my sickness, I now had almost sixty-five pounds of love crushing me…making my breathing a wee bit on the labored side.

The phone rang. Since it was in arm's reach I should have been able to answer it; however, since both arms were pinned under the blanket and the animals were ignoring the shrill ringing, I couldn't move enough to answer it. Finally, I managed to get one arm free.

"Hello." I wheezed.

You have been selected for a brief survey on toilet bowl cleaners."

Really? I answered the phone for a survey?! Grrrr!

My Pants Are Alive

Lying in bed one morning, I watched my cat Sox suddenly jump up on the chair where I had placed my pants. His laser focus zoomed in on a pair of jeans draped over the chair arm. He immediately started slapping at it, tussling with the jeans apparently trying to get at something.

I started to laugh, Sox glanced up at me. He gave me "that" annoying glance that only cats can do and continued to attack the pants ignoring me.

It suddenly dawned on me that *there might be* something in the pants that was causing him to slap the jeans into submission.

Just as I started to get out of bed, Sox pushed the jeans to the floor. Giving it a self-satisfied look, he proceeded to groom himself and ignore the jeans.

I picked them up, shook them, nothing fell out. Just marking up the play to a cat's whimsical fancy, I put the jeans on. As my right foot and leg were halfway into the jeans leg, I felt something by my foot…moving. Not a good sign.

I was too far committed not to push my leg all the way through the opening, hoping that I was pushing out whatever was in there.

Hopping around on one leg while trying to get my leg through the pants leg, a lizard plopped down on the floor and scooted off. I cursed. And, Sox? He continued to groom himself.

Cats!

Can I Stay Or Must I Go?

When you know you have a special skillset, you must use it or lose it. Apparently, one of my major skillsets is to annoy the cat...greatly.

Not owning a cat for many years, I was totally unaware that the slightest disturbance in their environment could cause a *major* disruption in and around their kitty litter box.

My adult rescue cat was particularly sensitive about *anything* that was disturbed in *his* room. Apparently I didn't acknowledge the rules of the domesticated cat when I brought him home.

Rule 1: The house belongs to the cat. You just live there as a guest and are to serve his every need. The fact that the house is in my name is irrelevant.

Rule 2: See Rule 1.

Recently I had received a number of boxes and put them in the cat's room. He wasn't happy about his space being invaded and didn't use his litter box in a tidy fashion.

The following week I organized the boxes so they weren't just tossed around the room. The cat did not attend the Martha Stewart School of Living, was unhappy about the new, improved area, and, again, didn't see fit to use his litter box the way it was designed to be used.

I learned my lesson. If I move one thing in *his* room, it needs to be left alone for forty-eight hours, and then life is good. Slowly I am re-arranging *his* room.

Sox…at his beck and call since 2012.

No Door Can Keep Me In

My screened-in backdoor now has plastic lattice attached to the inside of the door. The reason? My exuberant Malti-poo went through the screened door in a burst of excitement thinking she could catch a defiant squirrel who had the audacity to dance in front of her with no repercussions. She caught the last hair in his tail, surprising both of them. I can't have her plunging through the door whenever she feels like it. Thus, the plastic lattice.

I had let her out one morning, making sure the door was shut but not locked, I noticed through the window that Sox, my indoor cat, was carefully examining the door. Glancing around to see if I was anywhere near, he very genteelly put his paws on the door in an extended stretch and pushed a little on the door. He must have felt the door move slightly because this time he did a full body stretch against the door and it opened.

I immediately opened the kitchen door and roared, "Sox! Come back here!"

As cats are wont to do he turned back on the back porch with a disdainful glance at me, laid down, and licked his paws fully convinced he had done nothing wrong.

Cats!

The Cat Rub

I have a black and white cat named Sox. I'd said I own him but, as any cat owner knows, you never own a cat. They merely tolerate us because we know how to use a can opener and they don't.

After watching and laughing throughout the Sad Cat Diary video on YouTube with Sox, yes he occasionally gives me the impression he's paying attention to what I'm doing on the computer, I decided to rub his belly "exactly two times." And, unfortunately, he did exactly what the video said he'd do, "he bit the crap out of me, according to protocol."

Sox has been banned from laying on my desk while I'm watching cat videos now. Do I think it's had any sort of effect on him? Absolutely not! The cat now jumps up on the back of chair, almost giving me whiplash every single time, and watches the videos from there.

(Sigh) He is amused. Grrr, cats.

Animal Freedom Ride aka The Escape

When you have indoor animals, specifically cats, at some point they believe they are prisoners-of-war and are honor-bound in generational promises through the centuries that they should escape from their captors.

They plot and plan their escape while staring out the windows under the pretext that they are aloof creatures and don't need human companionship. It helps if there is a dog or two in the house to help them plan their freedom ride. This is also known as a conspiracy against their two-legged guardians who provide food, shelter, and water for them with nary a complaint. Well, okay, maybe a couple of complaints here and there but nothing to warrant an animal coup d'état.

While on the far side of my property, I looked back and discovered my back door swinging in the breeze. My Malti-poo, apparently a co-conspirator with the cat, had pushed the door open, bounded over to me, and tried to keep me otherwise engaged so I wouldn't notice the cat was now out in the yard.

Panicking, because the cat doesn't have front claws, I started to shout at the cat to "get back in the house." Yeah, like he understands English. He ran back inside when he saw me approaching.

There is now a lock on the back door…which Sox has now figured out how to unlock. Grrr!

Hide-and-Seek…Can You Count To Five?

My black and white cat Sox takes great delight in pretending to be a hidden lion in the jungle. Since I do not have live foliage in the house, he's taken to hiding behind boxes, burrowing under loose papers waiting to be shredded, and jumping on top of the refrigerator. Admittedly, it's a wee bit un-nerving to come into the kitchen, look up and see him peering over the top of the refrigerator.

Recently I had a fairly good size piece of wrapping paper that I had carelessly tossed on the floor. I was going to use it to stuff a box but just hadn't gotten that done yet.

Putting away a couple of things, I didn't notice the piece of paper following me. I heard a paper crunch sound, turned around, and didn't see anything except the paper on the floor. Brushing the sound off to my active imagination, I continued to put away a few odds and ends.

Out of the corner of my eye, I saw the paper move. I jumped. My first thought was something small was under the paper, like a mouse. Why this thought occurred to me when I had never had a mouse in the house was beyond me.

The paper moved again. Taking a deep breath to calm my nerves, I leaned over and carefully lifted up the corner of the paper. Sox sprang out, slapped my face with his paw, and took off. I screamed and almost passed out from fright.

That piece of paper has now been stuffed in a box.

Who, Me?

My Lhasa Apso Plop-Plop had recently ruptured his anal gland, was wearing a cone around his head, and had difficulty in jumping up on my bed at night. So being a good mama, I would scoop him up and place him gently on the bed.

Of course sometime during each night he would jump off the bed and then would bump against the bed for me to put him back up.

Normally Lhasa's weigh in the low twenty pounds, not Plop-Plop. He was bigger boned, built like a small fullback for the Southeastern Conference, and weighed twenty-seven pounds. It was like picking up a small heifer in the middle of the night.

After the cone came off, he discovered he could still wake me up and get me to put him on the bed by emitting a high pitched hum. I thought it was just because he was healing and he couldn't tolerate the pressure of jumping up on the bed until I came home in the middle of the afternoon and discovered the rascal was sleeping soundly on the bed.

I knew the dog fairies had not magically lifted him on the bed. The little bugger was jumping up on the bed in the daytime and then acting too sore to do it at night.

I have been manipulated by a dog.

Temporary Insanity

Dear Emma:

There is a new way for my two little dogs and my cat to show their love and affection to me first thing in the morning.

I love having them sleep in bed with me, a wee bit crowded but still enjoyable. They all get on and off the bed at some point during the night and thankfully only one needs assistance in getting back in bed.

They have now adopted a new ritual when I help Angel, the Malti-poo, get back into bed. She sneezes on me just as I am snuggling back under the covers. When she sneezes on me the other two also promptly sneeze. Two of the three animals deem it appropriate to sneeze…on me.

In fact, they have colluded and decided my head area needs to be sneezed upon. Sometimes it is a just a gentle mist of dog or cat fluid, but still unwanted and unwelcomed. Other times it is a full-on snort, requiring a tissue to remove said fluid off my face. Euuwww!

Any suggestions?

Signed,

Sharon – who's tired of a wet face in the mornings.

Dear Sharon:

Put your head under the covers as soon as you put your

animals on the bed. Duh!

Signed,

Emma

The Yo-Yo Syndrome

Manipulation of the human senses start with four legs and a furry coat. These creatures learn early on if they are imprisoned in a large, nice, roomy, and tastefully decorated home that it is their j-o-b to make sure the owner understands that they prefer to be outdoors.

They accomplish their mission by demanding to be let out the moment you decide to sit at the computer and work or the minute you take clothes out of the dryer and your arms are full or you decide to do deep breathing exercises to keep from screaming obscenities at them, having the neighborhood three blocks hear you, and possibly reporting you to the police.

When you let them out to enjoy nature, warm themselves in the sun, and do whatever it is these four-legged creatures do outdoors, you smile contentedly and go back to working. The moment you get thoroughly "in the zone," that's the exact moment they decide they need to come back indoors. It must be a genetically pre-disposed gene to alert them that you are now concentrating on something other than them.

This scenario plays out, in my household anyway, at least four times in the morning and afternoon. Of course, it doesn't help matters any that they receive a treat when they come back in every time.

Can you say "sucker"?

Interior Decorating With Toilet Paper

Please explain to me why cats have such a fascination with toilet paper. My black and white cat Sox periodically decides that the paper hanging from the roll in the bathroom is his to do whatever he likes. Makes no difference which way the paper is hanging, he helps it to escape from the roll.

As the sheets were fluttering down into the toilet bowl, apparently Sox was the only one who could hear the silent screams of "Help me, I'm drowning!" cries of the paper. Ever the vigilant cat, he endeavored to save as many sheets as he possibly could by dipping his paws into the toilet bowl and flinging them to safety…repeatedly.

There were wet sheets of paper who had made their new home on the bathroom walls, the shower curtain, the floor, some of them still preferred water and they ended up in the sink. Some sheets, tired from their swimming exertion, decided to rest on the edge of the toilet seat.

Meanwhile, Sox sat on the sink countertop licking his paws and pleased with his interior decorating skills.

I now shut the toilet lid.

Just Because You Tell Funny Church Stories Doesn't Make You A Christian Comedian

Apparently I Won't Be Saved Today

Moving to a new city, I decided to visit a local church. Several weeks later I received a telephone call.

"Hi, I'm Glenda with the Ooey-Gooey Church. We're coming to see you at seven tomorrow night and answer any questions you might have about Christ. Goodbye."

They were prompt. Welcoming in the two men and Glenda, I set out a plate of brownies. Unfortunately, my brownies had not turned out well, they looked like sludge from a septic tank. In all fairness, I was late getting home from work and didn't exactly follow the directions on the box.

One of the men, apparently deciding he was covered by the grace of God and wouldn't die, carefully inserted a gooey brownie in his mouth. He nodded politely. No else ate a brownie.

"So, what questions do you have for us about Christ?" Glenda had attended the Katie Couric School of Perkiness.

"Do you think the Virgin Mary spanked Jesus?"

They looked like Bambi in the headlights. I plunged ahead.

"On the pilgrimage when Jesus disappeared, why did it take his parents half a day to realize he wasn't with them?"

The pious folks from the Ooey-Gooey Church all turned pale, sweat was glistening on their faces, and I must have looked like the evil one.

"Ah, Miss Sharon, we need to go now. Another appointment," Glenda laughed nervously. "Hope to see you at church Sunday."

Wait! I still wanted to know the secret of water being turned into wine.

John the Baptist

Growing up in a small, sleepy town in Northeast Florida, there were only two things to do as a young adult. You could either go to church every time the doors opened or you could drink. If you were a Bapist and smart, you could figure out a way to do both.

Being a Presbyterian at the time, I took great delight in poking fun at the Baptists every opportunity I got. In school, starting about the seventh grade, all of the Baptist kids started evangelizing every opportunity they got. They were dedicated in their zeal to save souls for Christ. I'm guessing they had a contest running for who could save the most and, more importantly, bring them to church.

Years later, I was in Tallahassee enjoying an adult foamy liquid libation on the back deck of a popular eating establishment. A guy walked over to me and said, "Aren't you Sharon Buck from Palatka?"

To say my heart stopped is an understatement! As my brain was frantically scrolling through the Rolodex in my head to find some type of association with this guy in front of me and his name and hoping he wasn't a weird serial killer, I said, "Yes, I am and I'm sorry but I don't remember your name."

He grinned and said, "You probably knew me as John the Baptist. I 'baptized' sinners at Silver Lake."

We both laughed and reminisced about the friendly dunking contests the various church groups did at Silver Lake.

"What do you do now?"

"Oh, I'm still John the Baptist but now I 'baptize' people with beer. I own this place."

We celebrated to his success…with beer.

The Conversion

Last night I went to see a Christian comedian. While waiting for the performance to begin, I was telling funny stories to my friend.

Now, mind you, we were in a church and I was careful not to get out of line while telling these stories. Some of my stories are not necessarily ones you would or should tell in church...me being somewhat of a free spirit in my slightly younger days...or even last week.

In this particular church, it was a small one, everyone was sitting on padded folding chairs and I, being the ever observant person I am, had not really noticed that the folks sitting behind us had leaned forward to hear my stories...although I did hear a snort behind me from time to time. This is the South and a snort or two from folks is, unfortunately, quite common and, therefore, I paid absolutely no attention to it.

Anyway, my friend was laughing and encouraging me to tell more stories. So I continued merrily on. I told her the story about the hot tub and ended with the "Note to self: do not have lunch with a Baptist who thinks all containers of water are a baptismal font."

I very clearly heard the gentleman behind me say, "Amen to that, sister. Praise God."

I had forgotten we were in a Baptist church. Falling out of your chair laughing before the comedian started is not deemed good Christian etiquette.

Do-Re-Me

Feeling compelled one Sunday morning to attend church, I am not a regular go-er anywhere, I chose a non-denominational one to visit.

Prior to the church service, I recognized a local musician approaching a mid-twenties guy. He said, "How 'bout I play with you guys today? I can play with the best of them."

The younger guy shook his head no and said, "We'll stick with what we're doing."

The musician smiled and went back to his seat.

The younger guy bounced up to the stage area...okay, in church parlance, it's probably called something else so forgive me...and started to play his guitar and his backup ensemble, i.e., the church choir aka two women and another male singer, proceed to sing.

Now I knew why the local musician had asked if he could play with them, they were less than good. In fact, they were just flat out bad. I know God says make a joyful noise unto the Lord but, mercy, it sounded like cats fighting.

The younger guy, played the guitar slightly better than a beginner but his singing was horribly off-key. I'm tone deaf and have absolutely no sense of rhythm but I do have the good sense NOT to pretend to be a music director in a church.

On the comments section on the visitor card, I wrote, "Get

auto-tune for your choir and your music director."

I haven't been back.

The Pink Sock

Attending a church service with a friend, she decided we would sit down front…probably to keep me from escaping.

This was a very formal church where everything is extremely structured and left nothing to chance, not normally my type of church. I'm more of an energetic church type person.

Leaning over, I said in a sotto voice, "If the Holy Spirit shows up here, it will be by accident."

She wasn't amused.

Because we were sitting so close to the rare, sanctified pulpit area, I noticed the organ and the organist were turned a little sideways to the audience. Yes, I know they're actually called a congregation in a church but it's still an audience in my book.

I could see the organist's feet dancing over the foot pedals. While that kept me amused for a couple of minutes was that she was wearing a Nike sneaker on her right foot and her left foot only had a pink ankle sock on.

This wasn't just any pink ankle sock but noooooo. It was a neon pink sock that flashed merrily over the foot pedals with surprisingly manual dexterity. I was mesmerized by this display of a pink foot lightly touching a foot pedal and then scooting away to find another pedal.

Finally glancing up at the organist who was smiling in a knowing way at me, mouthed the words, "K-mart."

SHARON E. BUCK

I now own a pair of neon pink socks.

Walking on Water

Recently I was having lunch with two other girlfriends. One is a Baptist who always does the headache prayer before meals and the other is Catholic who does the sign of the cross at the drop of a hat. I eat while acknowledging the salt and pepper.

We were engaged in a spirited conversation when the Baptist suddenly said, "Sharon, you don't walk on water."

"Yes, I do." I replied smugly. "Technically, it's been shown and proven that there is always at least one molecule of water between our feet and the ground. Therefore, I walk on water."

I was laughing. The Catholic was horrified but starting to laugh and my Baptist friend, bless her heart, started shouting, "That's blasphemous! God will get you for that!"

"Do you really think God didn't know what he was getting when he made me?" I was still laughing.

My Baptist friend was still upset and thinking that she would insult me snapped, "You are a heathen!"

"Yes, but forgiven." I was feeling pretty righteous at this point. "And God has a sense of humor."

Fuming, she got up from the table and said, "I will pray for your soul."

"You need the practice and I need the prayer," I gleefully shouted after her. She refuses to have lunch with me anymore.

Huff and I'll Puff...
Until I Fall Over

I Don't Do E*x*e*r*c*i*s*e

It was the first of the year and I was determined to start a new exercise program. The chunky monkey of fat that had deposited itself around my waist, though no fault of my own of course, needed to go.

Being a wee bit older than those cute younger people usually gracing the exercise dvd covers, I was looking for someone who had a few wrinkles on their face, someone who had lived a little and probably had been around the block once or twice.

Scouring the big box stores and several of the more well-known internet sites, I finally decided on Jane Fonda's Trim, Tone, and Flex program. I knew she had sold millions of her exercise programs way back in the '80's and that meant she had "street cred." Yeah, I'm hip. I know what street cred means.

The program looked simple enough – upper body, lower body, and combination of upper and lower body. The package said the first two routines were twenty minutes each. Actually, they're twenty-five but who really cares about five minutes when you passed out at the ten minute mark?

The exercises look surprisingly simple…until you start to do them. I was huffing and puffing at the end of five minutes. This couldn't possibly be because I was so out of shape. No, it had to be that exercise witch's fault.

Deciding to uphold my title of computer geek, I know that none of us exercise except for our fingers on the keyboard. And that's good enough for me.

I Hate Jane Fonda

In the midst of my latest project, it occurred to me that I needed to exercise more. Sitting behind the computer does not for a healthy body make.

Being of a certain age, I didn't want to look like Jillian Michaels, do yoga with Rodney Yee, or even Sweating to the Oldies with Richard Simmons. I wanted a more mature female without looking like Harmonia the Amazon.

After careful research, and discovering that there was only one mature female in the exercise category, I decided on Jane Fonda's Trim, Tone, Flex DVD.

I had a mental flashback to the 90's when Jane came up with some ungodly exercise moves. Moves that stretched every muscle in my body and invoked much pain…pain I finally got rid of last week…decades later.

Summarizing that Jane couldn't possibly be doing those same moves now, I ordered the DVD for overnight delivery. I was excited! I was pumped to start my new exercise program!

Jane still looked gorgeous on the DVD. The moves looked pretty easy I thought while previewing the DVD. Excited, I immediately started working out with Jane.

I did great…for the first five minutes, then I was sweating like a pig in heat. Telling myself that the fat was melting away quickly, I continued to push myself. Apparently I was in a state of induced exercise shock. While watching Jane execute a very simple movement, I attempted to duplicate it. Turning sideways in a chair with and twisting the upper part of my body even further around caused me to lose my balance and I fell on the floor.

I now have two very LARGE black and blue bruises on my hiney cheeks and I can barely stand up and sit down without unbelievable pain. Forget about exercising anymore!

P.S. Jane, I hate you!

I Hate Yoga

Encouraged by a business coach who was in the throes of trying to lose weight but failing to share that priceless bit of information with me, I purchased DDP Yoga, aka Diamond Dallas Page former world wrestling star, and decided to become flexible. How that would help me in writing books was beyond me but, hey, I was paying big bucks for this coach and I figured she knew what she was doing. I was wrong.

Diamond Dallas is a big guy, very enthusiastic, and it was hard not to get caught up in his excitement…until the third exercise. I couldn't touch my toes, much less drop to the floor and do a modified cobra move. Pretending to be a snake was never on my top 100 things to do or be.

My muscles were screaming in agony, sweat poured off my face and down my body like Niagara Falls, I laid on the floor too weak to reach my cell phone and call 9-1-1.

The dogs were absolutely of no help. They thought I was going to play with them. The constantly nudging of their cold, wet, little noses is probably what revived me after what I thought was an hour but turned out to be only five minutes.

Staggering to my feet and looking at the tv, Diamond Dallas was proclaiming that with a little practice every day I could be flexible, build up my strength, lose weight, and be the kind of person that others envied.

I decided to try it one more day. If I thought Jane Fonda was bad, Diamond Dallas was Attila the Hun. I gave the DVDs away and

and now have a dartboard of him in my office. I hate him!

I Don't Like Pilates Either

Reading in a popular exercise magazine that Jennifer Anniston loved Pilates, how easy it was, how great it made her body look, blah, blah, blah, I decided to try it.

Ordering Mari Windsor's DVDs, I should have known how much of a challenge this was going to be when Mari didn't do all of her own exercises and, when she did, they weren't as perfect as those cute little girls doing them.

In fact, you could place a whip in Mari's hand, have her wearing a mask and a cape, and you would be begging for your life within ninety seconds. I couldn't even make it through five minutes of elongating my muscles with the rubber tubing.

Determined that THIS exercise program was going to work, I tried my darnest to get my arms and legs coordinated with Mari and her merry band of contortionists. Alas, it was not to be.

My hands accidently slipped off the handles of the rubber tubing and it slingshot itself across the living room and popped Angel, my Malti-poo, in the rear thus unleashing an ungodly scream that could be heard to South America. I didn't know dogs could scream. While trying to control myself between laughter and being horrified at what I had done, the phone rang. Attempting to get up off the floor and reach the phone on the coffee table, I knocked a vase of flowers over.

"Hello." I breathlessly answered.

"Are you okay? I heard a scream at your house." Neighbors in my neighborhood do pay attention to unwanted sounds emanating from houses and, while she was two houses down from me, I did appreciate her calling. I explained what happened.

"You might not to do that exercise thing anymore. You might hurt your other dog."

I don't like Pilates either.

The Exercise Ball

Watching a well-known actress on a talk show explaining the benefits of an exercise ball, I became overly enthusiastic and rushed out to purchase one.

Ignoring life-long warnings of a lack of balance, I somehow didn't realize that the ball is *round*. I sat on it for the first time and immediately was tossed onto the floor like a rag doll. There was nothing in the instructions that indicated this might occur. It was funny the first two times it happened. On the twenty-fifth time, I was considering puncturing the ball and letting all of the air out.

Determined not to let a sturdy beach ball rule me, I picked out the most difficult exercise to do on the instruction sheet. Surprise, surprise, I could actually do it! I tried the next most difficult exercise to do it and, again, I could do it. My confidence was building. I was high-fiving myself.

Feeling pretty darn proud of myself, I sat on the ball to prove that I had conquered the balance issue. Immediately, I found myself on the floor once again. Annoyed was an understatement.

I called a friend who is an exercise coach, explained what had happened, and asked the ever-popular question, "Why can't I sit on the ball without falling off?"

She laughed. "Some people just can't do simple."

There's a reason why she's not my exercise coach.

TV and Exercise

Not too long ago I bought an exercise bicycle with the ultimate goal of riding my way to excellent health while watching television. I figured I could do something enjoyable, like watching The Big Bang Theory, while doing something that was beneficial to my health but that I wasn't wild about doing, like exercising comfortably.

As with most things, I started out with good intentions. I set the resistance lever at the lowest point and proceed to pedal my way to nowhere. It was a lot of action but no forward motion…kind of like how my life felt at that moment.

The moment sweat started riveting down my face I could feel those unwanted inches sliding of my body into never-never land. Hooray! Those fat calories no longer had control over me.

After five minutes of hard pedaling, I knew that thirty minutes of doing this while watching a tv show was not going to happen any time in the near future but, for some unknown reason, I believed I was dropping pounds at the rate of one every minute I was bicycling. You can call it delusions of grandeur.

After discovering that I had only burned ten calories during my exercise routine, I was discouraged, mad, outraged, and just plain pissed off. It takes approximate 3,500 calories to make one pound. At the rate I was going it was going to take me seventy days or over two months to lose ONE pound!

It's now been two months since I first started riding my bicycle and I've gained a pound instead of losing it. Apparently my eating a chocolate bar while exercising...to keep up my energy level, mind you...added the weight.

I hate that exercise bicycle. I now call it the phat bike.

SHARON E. BUCK

I'm On The Seafood Diet…
I See Food and I Eat It

The Bacon Multiplier

I don't buy bacon very often simply because it disappears in my refrigerator. I am NOT one of those folks who has a refrigerator overflowing with food and condiments. I like a fridge that is clean, tidy, and one that I can see everything at one shot, which is why it's so frustrating not to find the bacon in the exact same spot every time.

Living alone, there is absolutely no reason why the bacon should go from the meat tray to the vegetable tray to hiding on each shelf. And, no, I'm not losing my mind or that absent-minded.

I swear, I think it roams the refrigerator at night.

Telling my friend about the bacon travels over lunch one day, she turned pale, her fork halfway to her mouth, and her eyes glazed over in horror. She carefully put her fork down and motioned for me to lean forward over the table so only the two of us could hear.

She looked around the restaurant and then whispered, "That happens to you too?"

I had goose bumps on me the size of Mount Everest and chills were running up and down my arms.

"Whh-whaat?" I stuttered.

"That happened to me all the time. I thought I was going crazy." She laughed nervously. "That's the real reason why I sold you the refrigerator."

Friends.

Bad Coffee Day

The other afternoon I met with two friends at the local coffee shop. Although the shop is a nationally recognized chain, it is not a high end coffee bar.

We were laughing and I ordered decaf with a shot of mocha, cream, sugar, and a shot of whipped cream on top. The two guys ordered coffee, black.

The girl behind the counter repeated my order perfectly. Then she turned to the guys.

"What do you want in your coffee?"

"Black."

"Black and what else?"

The guys gave each other a tolerant smile. "Just black."

Let me hasten to add that she's not new, she's been there for at least six months, and we go into that place about once a week.

Wes said, "Just black, the way I always drink it."

"Yeah, I got that. What else do you want in your coffee?" She enunciated each word slowly.

Steve grumbled, "Black."

"Yes, but what else do you want in your black coffee?"

The guys rolled their eyes.

"Just put two small cups on the counter and pour the coffee in. Then we'll tell you what else needs to be added."

She did that and the guys snatched up their coffees. She looked puzzled.

"That's how they want their coffee."

It was a bad coffee day.

Who Says I'm Fat?!

The other day I was sitting at my desk and minding my own business. The phone rang and caller id showed the number as V890 and a string of numbers.

"Hello."

"Hello. This is Jennifer and I am from Cambodia. I am here to help you with your weight loss because I know you are fat."

Say what?!!!!

Fat? Okay, I'm a couple of pounds over where I want to be but I. AM. NOT. FAT.

"What?" I was stunned to say the least.

"You are fat and we want to help you lose weight." The poor girl sounded very tentative; however, I AM NOT FAT.

"No, thanks." I slammed the phone down.

I was highly irritated and then I started to laugh. I know taking a picture adds ten to twenty pounds on a person. Maybe a phone call from Cambodia adds another forty to fifty pounds.

According to my friend Kirk, "Everyone's fat to a Cambodian."

Now where is my peanut brittle?

It's Five O'Clock Somewhere

My day is perfect. No one argues with me, I get things accomplished, I'm focused on my goals, I'm happy and calm, the dogs and the cat don't act they've started World War III…until I get out of bed. Then real life takes over my imaginary world.

I discover the cat's hacked up three hairballs the size of Texas on my clean clothes during the night. One of the dogs has pooped and peed in the hallway…right outside the bedroom door ensuring that I will see the surprise the moment I open the door.

The other dog is jumping around and acting like a maniac because he's sure he's going to die of starvation within the next thirty seconds if I don't feed him. Right. Now.

I have one hundred eighty-six emails warning me that someone has tried to gain access to my website BUT the wonderful spam software company I use to keep those delightful individuals out has decided they are going to double their renewal fee to continue to protect me.

There are three rejection emails from magazine publishers, one upset client because she can't figure out how to get into her website and somehow it's my fault, and my mother calling and demanding I take her to the grocery store THIS MORNING.

It's only 9:00 a.m. EST but I feel justified opening a cold frothy liquid libation because it's 5:00 p.m. in Dubai.

Sugar Is Energy – That's A Good Thing

I like to have a piece of candy after a meal…and sometimes in between. The candy bag is just tossed up on the kitchen countertop for an easy reach.

Watching the most recent Dancing with the Stars show, okay I have no sense of rhythm but truly enjoy watching others who do, a commercial popped up. I ran into the kitchen, grabbed a couple of pieces of candy, and rushed back to the living room.

During the next commercial, I repeated my dash-and-grab for candy routine. Popping a piece in my mouth and chomping down on it, I discovered a peanut butter taste in my mouth. Not being a big fan of peanut butter and being the astute individual that I am, I surmised I had picked up something else but what? The show started again and I watched until the next commercial. Priority focus, right?

Going back into the kitchen during the commercial break, I discovered I had grabbed and eaten a dog treat. Frantically, I started to read the ingredients on the package. It read like a shampoo list of ingredients…and these were supposed to be all natural treats. Ugh!!!

Note to self: turn on the kitchen light before grabbing candy off the countertop.

Punishment In The First Degree

A local store of a well-known coffee and donut chain has always had outstanding service. It was like the old TV show "Cheers" where "everyone knows your name." You could go in and the staff greeted you warmly, they knew how you wanted your coffee, and it was a well-organized breeze to get your coffee and a donut.

The owners sold it to a gentleman who owned five other stores of this same national chain. He immediately terminated the entire staff and replaced them with untrained, discourteous, and bored employees. These new hires couldn't find their way out of a paper bag with the top open.

Trying to order a cup of coffee was anything but easy and inevitably it was wrong. Plus, you never knew what the price was going to be. It ranged anywhere from a $1.09 to $3.26 during the 2-5 Coffee Happy Hour. There just wasn't any consistency in anything.

Our gang who met there every day became more and more frustrated with the service, lack of courtesy, and the inconsistency on the pricing. We decided to try another establishment for our afternoon get-togethers.

The Christian bookstore was not a viable since we all exhibited verbal heathenistic tendencies. Plus, we were overly exuberant in their way-too-quiet coffee area. McDonald's was just too far to go for coffee.

So, apparently, we don't have the sense God gave a goose and we now punish ourselves on a regular basis at – where else – the same coffee shop that can't get any two orders right.

Self-discipline

Recently I started a new diet...excuse me, a new lifestyle choice. This is a high protein diet for thirty days and I am supposed to eat five times a day. No sugar, no starches, no alcohol, no soda, no caffeine.

Day 1 – breakfast: bacon and eggs – not supposed to eat bacon because of the fat. I was hungry and did it anyway. Mid-morning snack – one slice of smoked salmon, probably half an ounce of protein. Lunch (at a local restaurant) – steak, greens, steamed cabbage, half and half tea. I wasn't supposed to have the tea but I gave up banana pudding so the tea works for me. Mid-afternoon snack – two celery stalks with peanut butter. Dinner – homemade split pea soup and water. No beer, no Coke, no tea, no dessert, no Dairy Queen ice cream.

This went on for five somewhat disciplined days. I modified my eating habits, mainly taking away my very beloved Cocoa-Cola and no dessert. At the end of five days I discovered my waist had dwindled down almost three quarters of an inch. This was very good news because now I can get into my less-than-fat jeans.

I figure in another week with another three quarters of an inch gone, I'll be able to breathe, and maybe move around even more comfortably, in my less-than-fat jeans.

Self-discipline, moderately done, is good for you.

There's A Reason Why I Don't Bake Cakes

After a night of frivolity and numerous liquid libations, I realized upon arriving home at three a.m. I had not made a birthday cake for the guy I was dating at the time.

Trying to be the best new girlfriend ever, I made an attempt to bake him a cake. Discovering the milk in the refrigerator was bad, hey, I was single and ate out all the time. I couldn't remember the last time I had checked the milk. I decided to make a milk run to the 7-11. They were closed. I tried several other places before hitting upon Walmart.

It was now four a.m. and I had to be at work by eight, I threw all of the ingredients into a bowl, mixed it up, and put it the oven. Apparently I had not leveled the cake batter out before putting it in the oven because it was now a very slanted chocolate cake. After being up all night and partying with him, I was sure he'd understand and, hopefully, be pretty pleased that I had made him a birthday cake.

After work I surprised him with the cake. He took one look at it and said, "My mother makes better cakes than that."

That was the last time I ever went out with him.

Protecting Santa's Cookies

It's three days before Christmas and I need to bake cookies for friends. Going to a very popular chain grocery store I discovered Santa had come early and put the cookies I wanted to bake on sale, two-for-one. Thrilled, I picked up ten packages of those cute little break off and bake cookies.

Standing in line to check out, several people engaged me in conversation making comments about how many cookies I would be baking. THEN someone noticed the different KINDS of cookie dough – midnight candy cane chocolate, triple chocolate chunks, pumpkin spice, turtle delights, and the ever popular white macadamia nut.

Suddenly those two seemingly sweet people standing behind me in line decided they needed to examine the packages a little closer. They snatched several of my packages and were carefully eyeballing the cookies and me.

I was now in a quandary. Do I create a scene in the checkout line demanding my cookie dough back or do I just snatch it out of these allegedly nice people's hands?

"May I have my cookies back?" I asked politely while mentally wishing the bad cookie fairy would burn all of their cookies they next time they decided to bake any.

Grudgingly, they handed me the cookie dough. As I was checking out, the cashier leaned forward and said, "You should have seen what happened about an hour ago. Two women started fighting and security was called."

Yes, Santa is alive and well…and protecting my cookie dough.

The Mollusk Conspiracy

Several years ago I was attending a local networking function. Running into a former boyfriend shortly after I had picked up a shucked clam, we proceed to catch up on each other's lives. Meanwhile, the clam I had so eagerly placed in my mouth, began to grow of its own accord.

It was a medium-size clam that grew to ginormous size inside my mouth. My eyes watered as I was trying to focus on what my former boyfriend was saying. Sadly, I have no clue what he said because I was trying to focus on swallowing the huge bi-valve in my mouth.

Unfortunately, this was not one of those events where one could discreetly remove the offending food morsel and no one would notice. Nope, the clam was now threatening to close my throat and probably cause me to suffocate in front of all these local politicians and business leaders…not the way I had envisioned my life ending.

My eyes continued to water, I tried to excuse myself, and finally jerked my head in the direction of the restrooms. I hurried off and there extracted the clam that had apparently come back to life in my mouth.

As I was catching my breath, I overhead two fine, well-known women chuckle and say, "Probably too much wine."

Seeing them later, I suggested they try the clams.

Can Fruitcakes Be Used As Door Stoppers?

Fruitcake has gotten a bad rap over the years. There is actually some delicious fruitcake out there. I know because I have eaten it.

As a joke several years back, my sister Gladys decided to buy an inexpensive, it was *really* cheap, fruitcake from a big box store and she mailed it to me for my Christmas present.

Opening it, I immediately noticed it was already dried out. In fact, I thought at first it had been mummified but upon closer examination I realized it had not reached that stage...yet. However, it was well on its way to being an artifact from King Tut's tomb.

Laughing, I realized she had read the same article I had in a popular magazine from several months earlier. The article told of one family's tradition of sending a fruitcake to each other for Christmas. They then re-wrapped it and sent it to another family member for the following year.

Realizing that she thought this was funny, which was a miracle in and of itself since she's not known for her sense of humor in our family, I mailed it back to her the following year.

We kept this up for five years before I received a note from her saying, "This isn't funny anymore. Stop sending the fruitcake."

Just because I'm the oldest and have a different sense of humor than she does, I mailed it back to her anyway the following Christmas. She doesn't really talk to me anymore.

Do You Like Kids?
...Baked or Fried?

Do You Want Fries With That?

I went to Comcast to pay my bill. I arrived at ten a.m. and the lobby was filled with people, including a screaming two-year old child.

Now, I enjoy many sounds in life…screaming children do not make the top one hundred on my list. However, I had once been a baby photographer and we had been trained on how to gain the confidence of a small child fast. The training had also included various techniques on how to get them stop crying.

Reaching back into the far recesses of my mind and calling forth those techniques to the forefront of my memory, I started making eyes at the baby. Right in the middle of an ear-shattering scream that could have been heard to South America and back, he stopped. A slight smile creased his face while his mother continued to ignore him.

I started playing with him as six other adults looked over gratefully at me. A couple gave me a thumbs up.

He suddenly reached out his arms for me to hold him. Oh, no! His food-stained shirt, grape-jellied face, and filthy little hands wanted to be held against my brand new Ralph Lauren green sweater? But, noooo!

Finally his mother turned around to look me. She nodded imperceptibly and then said, "Do you want to hold him?"

I shook my head no and said, "Bad back. Cute little one though."

The child continued to reach for me and started to wail after I paid my bill and was walking out the door.

I do have a way with children.

Happy Tummy

Playing happy tummy with my two and a half year-old great-niece Sophia recently, I tossed her on the couch and blew a raspberry on her tummy. Squealing with delight, we both laughed and then engaged in running around the house screaming and having fun.

Her mother Jordan didn't share our same exuberance and said in her mother voice, "Indoor voice." I grinned at Sophia. "Aunt Sharon." Grrr, I'd been tagged.

Sophia laughed and pointed at me and mimicked her mother, "Indoor voice, Aunt Sharon."

We proceed to play a little quieter, not much but a little bit. We were still tickling and chasing each other when Sophia came to a skidding stop, lifted up her shirt, laughed, and said, "I have a big tummy."

"Why do you have a big tummy, Sophia?"

"Because I eat veggies."

I leaned over to give her a big hug and I felt a tiny little finger poking in my tummy. Giggling, she said, "Why do you have a big tummy, Aunt Sharon?"

Admittedly, that question did catch me off guard but, hey, it's a small child, right? I laughed and said, "Beer."

She stepped back, grinned, and nodded her head. "Oh." And then said, "No more beer. Your happy tummy is big."

Note to self: No more beer.

The Blues Brothers Strike Again

Shopping with my niece and baby Emma at a big box store recently, it started to rain. While my niece ran through the pouring rain to get the van, I stood guard over the baby and the packages.

A very nice looking lady was running through the rain, stopped in front of me under the portico and asked if I needed an umbrella and if the baby was okay. I replied that I was just waiting on the van to come around. She said, "I'm a pediatric nurse and I always just ask about babies."

The thought occurred to me that maybe I didn't look like I belonged with the baby. While I was contemplating this thought, there was a growing number of other people standing under the overhang of the store trying to avoid drowning under the deluge of the rain. No one apparently wanted to get soaked going to their cars.

A guy in his mid-forties with an unkempt beard wearing a tee shirt and shorts sort of grinned at me and said, "How much for the leat-tle girl?"

He really drew out the word little and it kind of creeped me out. Having a brain flash of inspiration and recognition, I grinned and said, "The Blues Brothers, I know that movie."

He laughed and nodded. Others in the crowd laughed and nodded their heads also. Never under-estimate the power of a movie.

The Finger

My niece Jordan, her two and a half year old daughter Sophia, and I were in the garage working when suddenly Sophia decided to start screaming the word "no."

Jordan took Sophia's hand and went into the house. The screams of a very firm "no" increased to the volume that would deafen monkeys in the Amazon jungle.

A few minutes later Sophia opened the door and came out holding up her finger. I asked if she wanted me to kiss it. She looked at me quizzically and then nodded "yes."

"Where's your mom?"

"Baffroom."

"Okay, let me kiss your finger. Did you have a boo-boo?" Shaking her head no, she went back inside.

Looking up when the door opened, Jordan was laughing.

"What did you do when Sophia came out here?"

"I just kissed her finger. Why?"

"You should always ask a child where their finger has been before you kiss it."

My stomach roiled, the garage walls appeared to be breathing in and out, and I felt light-headed. Weakly, I asked, "Where had her finger been?"

Still laughing, she said, "In her butt...but she had her panties on so you're okay."

Note to self: Always ask a child where their finger has been before kissing it.

The Swipe

As a single aunt, never having children and not being schooled in the ways of small creatures, I was unaware of some of the more delightful attributes they exhibit when they have colds, coughs, or the flu.

Out shopping with my niece, her two and a half year old daughter Sophia was coughing and hacking. The gentle admonitions of her mother to "please cover your mouth when you cough" were ignored.

Ever the doting aunt, I said, "Do you want Auntie Sharon to hold you?"

A blood curling scream of "NO!" probably pierced the eardrums of monkeys in South Africa.

Deciding we needed to go home, we drove back with Sophia hacking, sneezing, and coughing the entire way. She very lady-like would swipe at her runny nose with her long-sleeved arm, thus removing any liquid that had the misfortune to dribble down her face.

Getting Sophia out of her car seat, she promptly sneezed a wet, gooey, and unwelcomed nose juice glob on the front of my blouse. I recoiled in horror and put her on the ground.

"Soph, you need to wipe your nose."

She immediately grabbed my sleeve, wiped her nose, then her face with it, and scampered into the house. Her mother laughed and said, "Welcome to my world."

I'm not sure I like small children any more.

Seriously. This Is My Life.

Boredom and No Rhythm

As a writer, I sit for long periods of time behind a computer. Sometimes I just sit and stare at the screen hoping words will just magically appear. That doesn't happen.

I struggle, I agonize, I plead, I curse, I do pretty much anything you can describe just to find the right word to use.

I get bored. There I've just admitted to something most working writers don't want the public to know. As fascinating as I find my own work, I do occasionally (gasp!) get bored with reading it.

This usually occurs about the time I've re-written a chapter, an article, for the umpteen time and I'm no longer in love with it.

Because I have the attention span of a gnat and I get bored so easily, I've devised other ways to amuse myself behind the desk. I've put my hair up in little top knots all over my head. FYI, this does not make for a lovely fashion statement in public – particularly if you have forgotten to remove the topnots.

I spin in my chair. It makes the dogs crazy to watch me spinning around so they join in the fun of chasing me in a circle while I just spin crazily. I stopped that after Angel threw up on my third time spinning around.

Then I stopped spinning altogether when I fell out of the chair in mid-spin. Not only was my ego somewhat bruised but so were my hine-y cheeks. I'm now learning how to play "wipe out" on my desk with my hands for amusement.

I Hate Snakes

I like being outdoors. I like being in nature. I like to feel the warmth of the sun on my pasty white skin. Even though I live in Florida, I am not a sun worshipper nor do I spend every waking moment at the beach; however, I do enjoy being out in my yard.

Inevitably though, something crazy happens almost every single time I go out in the yard.

I pick a rose and end up with an infection where the thorn pricked my finger or pulled up what appears to be a weed in the yard and end up with a very costly flesh-eating bacterial infection that has to be referred to the Center for Disease Control in Atlanta.

The latest episode was I had just gotten out of my car and locked the door when I saw this humongous yellow snake between me and the house. Everything in my body went ice cold. I couldn't get my key fob to open the car door.

Panicking, I managed to ease past my car and down the driveway. The snake proceeded to slither towards me. Throwing all caution to the wind, I ran up the front steps, punched my hand through the screen door and managed to get in the house. Slamming the door shut, I looked out and there sat that snake…on my front steps. Staring at me. I swear I thought it smiled at me.

I hate snakes.

It's A Conspiracy

Every time I really get focused on a project or writing or super involved on anything, a major distraction comes up. Every time. Without fail.

For example, I'm working on this short missive when I hear the dog's toenails clicking frantically on the hardwood floors from one end of the house to the other. Normally that much clicking indicates it's time for him to go outside. Okay, I'm smart, I got the message. I go to the back to let him out, he immediately sits down and refuses to go out.

Mumbling, I come back into my office and proceed to write again. The phone rings. While I normally turn the ringer off when I'm working, this particular morning I didn't. It was my mother calling. She's elderly and I needed to make sure she's okay. She's calling to thank me for the potato soup I made last night.

I start back on my writing when the light bulb goes out. Grousing, I replace the light bulb. Again, starting on my writing, I hear a knocking at my front door; thus, sending the dogs barking like banshees being let out of prison and having the cat flee to my desk top while having all paperwork scatter to the floors like leaves falling during the monsoon season.

It's either a conspiracy of the universe telling me to stop what I'm doing and do something else OR the universe wants to know how badly I want to complete something and do I have the fortitude to move ahead on it.

I'm thinking about moving to Jamaica.

Nature's Conspiracy

Pulling up in my client's driveway, I saw what appeared to be a dead snake laying there. Since some of nature's critters and I do not have a loving relationship, I debated whether to even get out of my car and go up to her front door.

Throwing all caution to the wind, I carefully eased out of my car. I let my purse dangle down to my ankles, keeping a barrier between me and the snake in case it decided to attack me.

Giving the snake a wide berth, I was in the process of backing up to her front door when that dog-ugly snake raised its head. Now, keep in mind, I have a very healthy respect for snakes. This one looked like it might a rattlesnake and I was taking no chances. I backed up to her front door even faster.

My client opened the door after my frantic ringing of her doorbell. I told her about the snake, she walked out, looked at it, and said, "Oscar, what have I told you about scaring people?"

We went back into her house. I did the computer work and came back out. The snake just laid there, faking his demise until I walked around him once again. He raised his head and I swear I think he winked at me.

I really don't like snakes!

The Brain Flu

Do you go through the angst of asking yourself too many questions? Of course not! It's just me and I know it's a conspiracy of the Universe.

Those stinking stars, moons, comets, black holes, whatever collude with each other so that it confuses the natural wave pattern in my brain. This causes me to ask way too many questions and bogs down my allegedly normal clear thinking process.

Questions that block me from progressing forward in my day-to-day life include:

- What kind of Dairy Queen Blizzard do I want today?
- Why does sweat cause weight loss? I mean, if I don't sweat, can I still lose weight?
- How is it other writers can crank out twelve pages a day on their book and I can barely get one page done?
- Do you think angels fly in formation around you or do they put you in the middle and charge through the day hoping you won't escape from them?
- Why does sticking your finger in a very foamy frothy liquid libation cause the foam to disappear?

And forget the why questions. They're just an endless loop with no answers. Somehow I get caught up in that...on occasion...well, maybe every day.

So my question for today is: why is there a ying and a yang when I can't find the balance in my life?

Paying Homage

I don't know about you but I have to pay homage to the washing machine about once a month with a sock. The sock is offered up as a way to keep the machine going; otherwise, inevitably, somewhere weird happens and I have to call a repair person out. A sock seems like a small price to pay to keep the machine going.

I've tried pinning socks together to keep one from wandering through the bowels of the washing machine and probably through the drain pipe. It doesn't work. The socks find some strange way to unpin from each other, leaving the sticky end of the safety pin to stab me in the finger when moving the laundry from the machine to the dryer.

I've tried rolling the socks up into a ball, that doesn't work either. They are very adept at separating from each other. Mind you, if I don't roll them up in a ball, they still find some way to get all botched up together. It's a conspiracy.

It's only my socks, mind you, that this happens to…no one else in the family has to make homage to the washing machine.

I have only one question: WHY ME?! And, where are the odd socks going?

Sticky Tape

With the New Year starting, I decided to put up a year-at-a-glance wall calendar. I carefully selected the one I wanted at a big office supply store.

Gleefully congratulating myself on how organized I'm going to be this year, I didn't think about *how* I was going to attach the rolled up calendar on my office wall.

That calendar had a mind of its own. It didn't want to un-roll and then when it did, it immediately did the football maneuver of hit-the-ground-and-roll.

Not willing to pound nails or put decorative tacks in my wall, I tried putting rolled up packing tape on the backside of the calendar and pasting it on the wall. That came un-done with the speed of a shuttle taking off for Mars and almost broke my nose in the process.

Cutting the clear packing tape into sections and then taping them to my jeans, I envisioned the strong possibility that I could hold the calendar in place with one hand while taping the corners and edges with the other hand. It never occurred to me that the tape would stick to my pants making the pieces difficult to remove. And I didn't realize that the tape would wad up in sticky bunches and be worthless in trying to put it on the calendar edges.

Finally I got the calendar secured to my wall when I strange sounds from my dogs. They had both walked on the wadded up sticky tape and were merrily bouncing down the hallway shaking their paws trying to get it off.

Note to self: pick up sticky tape Note to self: pick up sticky tape before it gets on the dogs' paws. It's a bear to remove without getting bit.

The Beard Whisperer

Living in a small town out in the middle of nowhere with the median income under the U.S. poverty line, it's always exciting to be asked out on a date with the expectations of being taken to a larger city for dinner and a movie.

Recently Joe (not his real name) asked me out. Now I've known him for a good many years, he's been divorced for the third time in four years, and he usually wears a closely cropped beard which looks really nice on him.

I hadn't seen him in several months when he called, he asked me out, and we agreed to meet at the Park and Ride lot. He stepped out of his truck and into my car…along with his beard that now touched his chest.

Within five minutes, he pulled out a baby blue hairbrush out of his pocket and started brushing his beard as he continued to talk about his ex-wife for the next twenty-five minutes.

Now I've dated some interesting men but never one that ever, ever brushed his beard continuously. What was even more unnerving was that he *talked* to his beard. Yes, he was saying affirmations to his beard.

"My beard is soft. My beard grows long and is healthy. I treat my beard well."

To be honest, I couldn't wait for the date to end. And the answer is no, I haven't been out with him again.

The Pregnancy Bet

My cousin Madison was pregnant and we were all anxiously waiting to find out if she was going to have a little girl or a little boy. Family members were taking bets as to which sex the new baby was going to be.

My aunt and I were totally convinced that it was going to be a little boy. We based our decisions upon the way Madison seemed to be carrying the baby.

My husband, a professional chef, bet both of us five dollars that it was going to be a little girl. His reasoning? He simply chose opposite from the two of us.

Madison *finally* posted the photos on Facebook showing that it was going to be…a little girl.

My aunt sent a text to both me and my husband saying, "Groan! We owe Sam five dollars."

Sam immediately texted back, "Pay up! LOL"

Since I take care of the finances in our family, I texted back, "Just take the five dollars out of your wallet and then put it back in there. LOL"

Now THAT'S funny. My aunt still owes him the five dollars.

The Cone of Silence

My friend Allegra and I get together for lunch about once a week. She is a former city commissioner and I'm a writer. Because we both run around, we come across some rather interesting tidbits of information. We frequently share that information with each other over lunch at a local diner.

Since small towns, and ours in particular, are known for spreading rumors, we rarely share information that couldn't be repeated in front of a newspaper reporter.

One recent day, she dropped into our favorite booth with a loud whoosh. She leaned forward over the table in a conspiratorial matter, grabbed a napkin, fluffed it out, indicated I should grab the other corners of the napkin, and said, "You're not going to believe this."

About that time, our favorite waitress Lu-Lu was walking by, backed up, looked at us with that oh-my-god-what-are-they-doing-now look, and cautiously asked, "What are ya'll doing?"

"It's the Cone of Silence," explained Allegra.

"Ah, what?"

"It's from Get Smart," I said laughing. "You know, Maxwell Smart and the Cone of Silence."

As a blank look crossed her face, it occurred to both me and Allegra at the same time that, depending upon your definition of middle-age, we're either slightly north of that number or right in the middle of it. Regardless, Lu-Lu who is a twenty-something gal, rolled her eyes, and said, "Ya'll really ain't right today, you know that?"

At another table, one of the lawyers looked over at us, we still had the napkin Cone of Silence up, grinned, and said, "Call me when the guys in little white coats come to get you."

Apparently folks in our hometown don't appreciate the importance of the Cone of Silence.

The Garden Dance

I'm not wild about gardening. Yes, I am fully aware it is almost un-American to admit this. Every time I work out in the yard something weird happens.

A flesh-eating bacteria noshed on my finger one time. That little episode was over one thousand dollars and not being to use my left hand for six weeks.

Then there was the time I brushed a tree trunk getting some type of slime-y goo on my arm and causing a red-dot, itchy rash to break out.

Reluctantly, I finally decided to mow the yard when I could no longer see my Malti-poo bouncing up and down in the grass. I was yanking on the cord to start the mower when I looked down and saw what appeared to be two black snakes crawling up my legs. I screamed, jumped away from the mower, and turned it over, spilling gas all over the ground.

I continued to scream and dance around when I suddenly realized it was the drawstrings from my shorts dancing up and down on my legs. I had not tied them and they were swinging wildly with each move I made. In my defense, I wear trifocals.

A weekly lawn service now maintains my yard.

The Hot Tub

Years ago, in my wild and crazy youth…okay, they haven't ended, they've just slowed down a wee bit…I used to engage in hot tub parties. These were not the wild and woolly stories you normally hear about. We just enjoyed the hot water and enjoyed a cold foamy frothy liquid libation, no naughty stuff, no hanky panky.

I was telling a friend about the time someone inadvertently let a bottle of peppermint schnapps slip through her fingers, a cardinal sin, and it sank to the bottom of the hot tub. We were all trying to find the sunken bottle with one hand while holding our drinks up in the other hand. No point in spilling anything other than water in the hot tub. Finally the bottle was found and the merriment continued.

Recently I was invited to a party involving some of these same people. I haven't seen them in a number of years. While flattered to be invited to the party, I was somewhat reluctant to drive two hours one way to attend the party.

I was expressing my thoughts to my friend and she brightly exclaimed, "You've been saved from your wanton ways. God snatched you up from hot tub madness."

Note to self: do not have lunch with a Baptist who thinks all containers of water are a baptismal font.

The Nickel

Receiving a new order of my first fiction book, I was delivering them to friends. They were just as excited as I was about the books.

All of the hard work, time, energy, and effort is now available for the world to see. The good news is that people are willing to pay for it!

I had my book priced at $9.95, a fair price I thought for my first fiction novel. People eagerly wrote me checks for the book. I was delighted.

Delivering *A Dose of Nice* to my buddy Kirk at the school board, he and I engaged in conversation. Kirk is one of those people you just can't help but laugh with on his stories. They're always funny and usually involve his cat Bigby.

Kirk and I both have a somewhat skewed perspective on life and we laugh a lot when we're together. In short, we're both a wee bit on the quirky side. I prefer the term "delightful character", Kirk prefers the term "genius." We'll go with genius.

We were sharing humorous stories and laughing. Finally, after about fifteen minutes, I said I had to go and deliver more books.

Kirk wrote me a check and said, "Bigby said to tip you a nickel for delivering the book."

Friends! LOL

The Panda Bears

On the wall in my office I have a 2009 Chinese calendar showing panda bears sniffing flowers and looking cute. I love pandas. There is something just so whimsical, happy, and loving about them.

Periodically I shoot videos in my office for my various websites. I always have several people review the training videos to ensure they make sense to non-techie people. Two people said the most recent video was fine. The third friend said, "Why do you have a calendar up from 2009? It makes your video look really dated."

I had never noticed that. I changed the calendar to the most recent one, re-did the video and sent it out to the same three people to review. The first two said again it was fine. The third friend said, "You have a sexy girl behind you and it detracts from your message."

After attempting to explain the girl was standing on a bridge and it wasn't about a pretty girl, it suddenly dawned on me. It was irrelevant what the actual calendar looked like if the only thing someone could see from the video was a pretty girl.

I put the panda bears calendar back up, typed the correct year on a piece of paper, and carefully taped it over the 2009 year. I showed the new video to my observant friend.

"I know you changed the year on the calendar but it looks good now."

You can't go wrong with pandas in a video.

Marketing Books

On Saturday I did a video book trailer presentation to a writers group.

Because I was lazy and didn't want to schlep my laptop with me, I had called the library the day before to confirm they had everything I needed. I was assured they did. Well, yes, they did but…in the course of setting up the library's laptop, I discovered it was woefully slow, had software on it that was more than ten years old, and it wouldn't connect with their projector.

They brought out another laptop. This one was older, slower, and worse than the other one. I mentally chastised myself for not bringing my laptop where everything was brand new, speedy, and worked properly.

I did the power point presentation which, while incredibly slow, did work. Unfortunately, I kept having to go out to the internet and find the videos I was using to demonstrate my book trailers.

Ironically enough, the only videos I could get to play were mine. The others just seemed to freeze up and all of the videos were on a very popular, well-known video site.

Judy, one of the writers who I had planned to feature her book trailer, laughingly shouted, "How come your videos are the only ones you're playing?"

"Marketing, Judy, marketing." The crowd roared with laughter.

Make lemonade out of lemons.

It's Just Lunch, People!

Do you ever have those days where you know you didn't graduate from the Katie Couric School of Perkiness? Yep, me too.

Recently, I was having a very rough morning. Being single and a writer, a double whammy in terms of living an active lifestyle, I felt the need for companionship for lunch.

After calling several friends for lunch and being turned down, I was annoyed. It was only nine-thirty in the morning.

"Humph," I grumbled. "How could they already have lunch plans?"

The next two people also declined my invitation. The sixth person kind of laughed and then said no. I exploded on this D-list friend.

"Why not? I've called five other people and no one wants to have lunch with me today."

She laughed. "You sound like you are beyond stressed and when you are stressed you are, ah, how can I say this nicely, intense." A slight pause then, "Honey, you are scary when you are intense and I don't want to have lunch with when you're like that."

I felt deflated, and although appreciative that someone finally had the courage to tell me the truth, I marked her off my list of friends. I ate alone that day.

Always Be Prepared

I like to take long, steaming hot showers in the early evening when it's still light outside. I relax as all of the garbage from my day flows from my body down into the drain. I totally zone out and am only vaguely aware of my surroundings until that noise-maker dog of mine decides to let loose with her yapping indicting something is seriously wrong.

Wrapping a towel around me and putting my glasses on, dripping water with every step, I have to check the back and front doors to make no one is trying to break in. She does this about once a week and never on the same day or at the same time. It's annoying.

Last week as I was once again luxuriating in the shower, the dog starts with her incessant yapping that went into the full-blown "Danger, Will Robinson, Danger!" barking. I jumped out of the shower, grabbed the towel, and went barreling down the hallway to the front door, cursing all the way. I had just barely put the towel in front of me when I yanked the curtain back on the door fully expecting to see a cat sitting by the door taunting the dog. It was a ten year old Boy Scout with his mother standing behind him. All of our eyes popped wide open.

I shouted, "Come back in ten minutes and I'll buy whatever it is you're selling."

He's never come back. Gee, I can't imagine why.

The Swearing In

Recently all of the former city commissioners were voted out of office and replaced with new ones.

Townspeople, family, and friends convened at the local auditorium for the swearing in ceremony.

The former chief justice of the Florida court system was there to swear in the new candidates.

The City Clerk had carefully placed the agenda on the podium so everyone could follow the script. Everything appeared to be perfect.

The outgoing commissioners and mayor all said a few words and moved off the stage. The chief justice called for the new mayor to come forward. He did so along with twenty members of his family and friends.

The chief justice looked solemn and said, "Before we swear in the new commissioners, we need a Bible."

It looked like Bambi in the headlights. Everyone looked around and apparently none of the new commissioners had thought to bring their own Bible with them. This had been the custom on all previous swearing ins.

"Does anyone in the audience have a Bible with them?" asked the chief justice, a bemused look on his face.

The City Clerk whipped out her cell phone and found a Bible image. The swearing in ceremony took place with the new mayor placing his hand on a cell phone.

Technology reigns.

The Exorcist Strikes

I was so proud of my new orange red Toyota. It got great gas mileage, was easy to drive, and comfortable to ride in for long distances.

Going in for my first oil change, I noticed the young guy look at my tag and then shake his head no. He went over to the shop manager, said a few words, and pointed at my car. The manager looked at my car then back at the young mechanic, laughed and called someone over to finish the oil change.

A couple of days later I had a flat tire on my brand new car. I wasn't happy and called for local roadside assistance to come and change the tire. The guy walked behind the car to get the license number, stopped, looked over at me, and said, "Lady, I can't work on your car. You'll have to call someone else."

"Why?" I was perplexed.

"Because I'm a Christian. Your car tag says exorcist on it, your car is red, and this is the work of the devil. I can't work on it."

"What?!" Looking at the car tag carefully, I realized it said XUR 666.

I kept that car and tag for ten years. It was amazing how many mechanics would not work on that car.

Truth in Advertising

Deciding to splurge on some new towels, I decided to go with a designer name…in a fancy, upscale store…in a much larger city than I live in…an hour away.

I was excited. The last towels I purchased came from a large box store that is in probably every town in America. Not saying that those weren't nice, they were, but they wore out fairly quickly.

I wanted a towel that was luxurious, soft, and would absorb every drop of water on my body. Convinced that a designer name would provide all of these requirements, I was almost giddy with my purchase. Washing and drying them according to the directions, I couldn't wait to dry myself off with the new towels.

Stepping out of the shower, I delighted in how the towel felt against my skin. It felt so good. I felt like a new person. The cares of the day had been flicked away like the water on my skin from my new towel. I was ecstatic and mentally high-fiving myself on my great new purchase.

Going through the kitchen, I noticed water on the floor. Since I was going to wash my new towel again, I put it on top of the spilled water. I totally expected it to absorb the water like a paper towel.

This was apparently an unrealistic expectation on my part. It did not absorb the water…at all.

Upset, I called the store, explained the situation, and fully expected to receive a refund. Instead, the snotty salesclerk informed me, "Ma'am, those towels are for the human body. May I suggest you use paper towels for your liquid spills, not the (insert designer name) towels?" Click.

I did return the designer towels and went back to the big box store and bought Martha Stewart towels.

Ya'll Ain't Right

My friend Allegra and I were having lunch at our favorite local eating establishment and, as normal, we were laughing and telling stories.

I was telling her a story about the time I and some friends were relaxing in a hot tub drinking peppermint schnapps. Because the hot tub was so hot and the weather was so cold we were blowing smoke "doughnut holes" in the air.

She laughed, "I had visions of a group of non-smoking adults exhaling frosty doughnut holes in the air." She was laughing so hard, she couldn't finish her meal. Our favorite waitress Lu-Lu kept popping over to hear the stories and was laughing with us.

As one funny story lead into another hilarious story, we stopped eating and kept laughing. Who cares about food when you can laugh with a friend?

Another of our favorite waitresses Karen came over and to see what we were up to.

Laughing with us, she said, "I don't think God wants ya'll back."

We were laughing so hard that we were about to fall out of the booth when Lu-Lu, wiping the tears from her eyes said, "Ya'll ain't right."

FUN, HUMOR & LAUGHTER

ABOUT THE AUTHOR

Sharon E. Buck lives in Northeast Florida and tries to make as many people as possible to laugh out with her short stories and humorous murder mystery novels.

Visit Sharon's website at www.SharonEBuck.com.

Follow Sharon on Facebook www.facebook.com/sharonebuck or on Twitter @sharonebuck

www.ingramcontent.com/pod-product-compliance
Lightning Source LLC
Chambersburg PA
CBHW071300040426
42444CB00009B/1805